Hat Tricks Count

A Hockey Number Book

Written by Matt Napier and Illustrated by Melanie Rose

Special thanks to Craig Campbell from the Hockey Hall of Fame.

Text Copyright © 2005 Matt Napier
Illustration Copyright © 2005 Melanie Rose

All rights reserved. No part of this book may be reproduced in any manner
without the express written consent of the publisher, except in the case of brief
excerpts in critical reviews and articles. All inquiries should be addressed to:

Sleeping Bear Press

310 North Main Street, Suite 300
Chelsea, MI 48118
www.sleepingbearpress.com

© 2005 Thomson Gale, a part of the Thomson Corporation.

Thomson, Star Logo and Sleeping Bear Press are trademarks
and Gale is a registered trademark used herein under license.

Printed and bound in Canada.

10 9 8 7 6 5 4 3 2 1

Library of Congress Cataloging-in-Publication Data

Napier, Matt.
Hat tricks count : a hockey number book / written by Matt Napier ;
illustrated by Melanie Rose.
p. cm.
Summary: "Using numbers, hockey's famous people, teams, history, and rules
are introduced. Topics include Wayne Gretzky, Hat Trick, Olympic gold medals,
and hockey sticks. Each number topic is introduced with a poem and includes
side-bar expository text with detailed information"—Provided by publisher.
ISBN 1-58536-163-1
1. Hockey—Juvenile literature. 2. Number concept—Juvenile literature.
3. Counting—Juvenile literature. I. Rose, Melanie, ill. II. Title.
GV847.25.N35 2005
796.962—dc22   2005005963

To my grandparents, Nana Shirl and Papa Jim,
who never missed a game.

MATT

∽

For all the hockey fans out there, big and small.

MELANIE

As a special tribute to the North American origins of the game of hockey,
we have chosen to use the Canadian spelling of selected words.

Can you find these words? How many did you correctly guess?
Check your results against the answers on the last page.

Wayne Gretzky is remembered as "The Great One" and is considered by many to be the greatest player to ever play the game. His number 99 is the only number to be retired across the entire National Hockey League (NHL). This means no other NHL player will ever be able to wear number 99 on his jersey. Individual teams also retire the numbers of the best players to lace up their skates for the team, but 99 is the only number to be retired league-wide. The number that has been retired by the most teams is the number 9. Gordie Howe, Bobby Hull, Maurice Richard, and Johnny Bucyk are among the hockey legends who have had their number 9 retired by one or more teams. The Toronto Maple Leafs also honour Ted Kennedy's number 9. Other famous retired numbers include Guy Lafleur's number 10 and Marcel Dionne's number 16.

Gretzky began his NHL career with the Edmonton Oilers and then played for the Los Angeles Kings and the St. Louis Blues before retiring as a member of the New York Rangers. The Rangers are an "Original Six" team—one of the first six teams which made up the early NHL. The other teams are the Montreal Canadiens, the Toronto Maple Leafs, the Chicago Blackhawks, the Detroit Red Wings, and the Boston Bruins.

one

1

1 When you think of hockey numbers should come to mind.
The Great One is his nickname.
He wore the famous "99."

2 goalies stand guard at opposite ends,
determined to make each save.
With tremendous skill and a little luck
a shutout is what they crave.

No matter the age group, skill level, or gender, a goalie has one job—to stop as many shots as possible. If a goalie lets in no goals in a game we say that he got a shutout, meaning he shut the opponents out of his net entirely. There have been many great goalies to play the game and record lots of career shutouts—Glenn Hall, Jacques Plante, Patrick Roy, Martin Brodeur, Ed Belfour, and Dominik Hasek, to name a few. George Hainsworth holds the record for the most shutouts in one season with 22! But one goalie stands above the rest in the shutout department—Terry Sawchuk. For more on this great goalie, check out number 100!

two

2

Although its origins are debated, the term "hat trick" in hockey was most likely adopted from the sport of cricket, which used the phrase to acknowledge a player who took three wickets with three consecutive balls. The story goes that the first cricket player to accomplish this feat was given a new hat by his team. Now, when a player scores three goals in a hockey game, fans throw their hats on the ice in celebration. This act probably has its origins in a promotion sponsored by a Toronto hat salesman, Sammy Taft. In 1930 Taft offered a hat to any player who scored three goals in a single NHL game in Toronto. Wayne Gretzky, who managed to amass 10 three-goal games in the 1982 season, holds the current single-season record for most hat tricks scored. Now we can all take our hats off to that accomplishment!

three

3

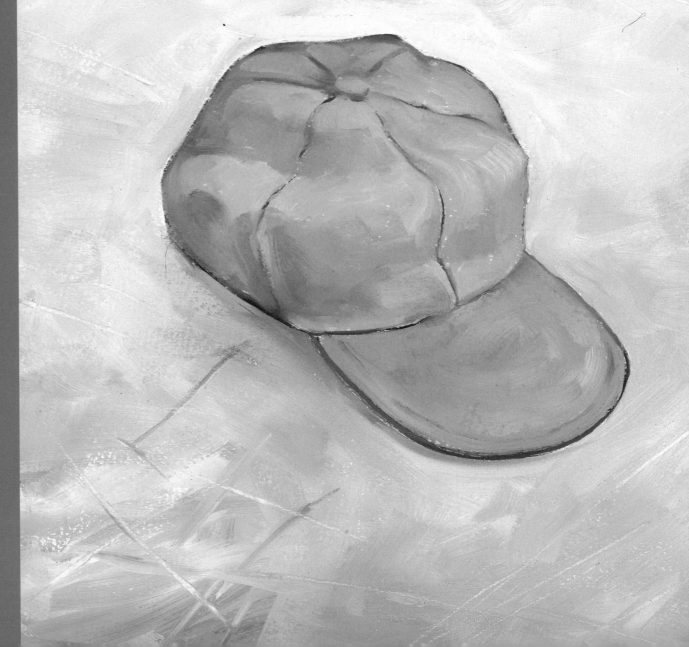

When one player scores 3 goals in a game
a brand new fan might ask
"Why are hats being tossed on the ice
in honour of this task?"

Few players have done as much for the sport of hockey as Jean Beliveau. While wearing the number 4, Beliveau won 10 Stanley Cups with the Montreal Canadiens. Beliveau served as captain of the Canadiens for 10 years and with him on the roster between 1955 and 1959 Montreal became the first team ever to win four Stanley Cups in a row (they went on to win a fifth consecutive cup in 1960). Fans, who remember him as "Le Gros Bill," say Beliveau was, and still is, one of the classiest ambassadors the game has ever seen. Testament to this is that in 1994 Beliveau was the first hockey player ever offered the post of Governor General of Canada, a position he turned down to spend more time with his family.

Other famous hockey "**4**s" include Bobby Orr, who not only is remembered for wearing the number 4, but also is the only player to win four major individual trophies in one year—the Hart, Norris, Conn Smythe, and Art Ross. Also, Bob Gainey of the Montreal Canadiens won four Selke trophies as the best defensive forward in his career, more than anyone else.

He wore the number **4** with pride
on red and white and blue.
Jean Beliveau is a hero still
to Hab fans through and through.

four

4

If a player scores a goal by shooting the puck through the goalie's legs, it's common to hear someone say "he went five-hole on that shot!" Goal scorers are always looking for new ways to trick goalies into leaving openings to the net, but goalies have been known to use slight trickery as well. Some goalies have the insides of their pads painted white so against the white ice it looks like there is more space to shoot the puck into the net!

Also, Mario Lemieux is the only player to score five goals in a game in five different situations—even strength, short-handed, power play, penalty shot, and empty net.

five
5

5 is for one of the openings
where a player can score a goal.
The space between the goalie's pads
is known as the 5-hole.

Sticks are very important to the sport of hockey—without them players could not score goals! But if used improperly sticks can also be dangerous. A player can use only his shoulder to check another player. If he uses his stick the referee will call a cross checking penalty. Also, a player must not touch another player with her stick if it is above shoulder height, or else she will get a high sticking penalty. The referee will also call a hooking penalty if a player uses his stick to "hook" onto another player to try to slow him down.

Hockey is a very fast game and the referee has to be sharp to make sure he calls penalties when a player breaks the rules. However, some players break the rules more often than others—in fact some players are best remembered for their propensity to get in trouble. Dave "Tiger" Williams holds the NHL record for most penalty minutes in a career, with 3,966. Other "tough guys" include Marty McSorely, Tie Domi, and Dale Hunter.

Each of these penalties are usually two-minute infractions, meaning the offending player must spend two minutes in the penalty box unless the other team scores a goal on their powerplay. Roughing and interference are also both two-minute penalties. The referee may call a misconduct if the player's action deserves more than two minutes.

six

6

Cross Checking

Misconduct

High Sticking

Hooking

Cross checking, high sticking, and hooking
are bad things to do with sticks.
Two minutes for each of these penalties
will all add up to **6**.

Roughing

Interference

There is little doubt that Canada and Russia have historically been two of the most competitive hockey nations in the world. Since ice hockey became an Olympic sport in 1920, no other team has won more than two gold medals—Canada and Russia have each won seven. However, there is some debate over these numbers as the "Unified team" which was comprised of players from countries in the former Soviet Union won the medal in 1992, so some people make the case that Russia has in fact won 8 gold medals. Also, the Canadian and Russian under-20 world junior teams have both won far more international junior titles since 1974 than any other team.

The number 7 represents two hockey-rich strongholds. Only Canada and Russia can claim to have won 7 Olympic golds.

seven

7

The 1972 Summit Series was played between the best players from Canada and the Soviet Union. In the eyes of many fans it was supposed to be a Canadian blowout as the team boasted many of the best players in the NHL. Since there were no Soviets in the NHL, none of the Canadian fans had heard of the Soviet players and most assumed they were no match for the Canadian squad. In the first game, however, the Canadians were left shocked as the Soviet Union won 7-3 in Montreal. The rest of the series was hard-fought and Canada faced elimination in each of the last three games. Paul Henderson's goal in game 8 is probably the most famous goal ever scored in Canadian hockey history. The series was an eight-game contest, but because one of the games was a tie and the Soviets had scored more goals in the series, Canada had to win the eighth and final game—a tie and the Soviet Union would be victorious.

Much of the Soviet team's success can be attributed to the unbelievable goaltending of Vladislav Tretiak, who went on to dominate international play for the next 12 years. Tretiak was inducted into the Hockey Hall of Fame in 1989.

eight

8

Game 1

Montreal

Game 2

Toronto

Game 3

Winnipeg

Game 4

Vancouver

me 5

oscow

Game 6

Moscow

Game 7

Moscow

Game 8

Moscow

These teams battled each other
back in 1972.
It took Canada **8** games to win
when Henderson's puck snuck through.

Known simply as Mr. Hockey™
while wearing the number **9**,
it was a thrill to watch Gordie Howe™ skate by
and shoot the puck across the goal line.

Gordie Howe didn't just play hockey, he *was* hockey—Mr. Hockey,™ to be exact. Many experts say no player has ever been as dominant physically, mentally, and skillfully as Gordie Howe was in his career. Not only could he score, he could pass, body check, and was one of the toughest players in the game. On top of that Gordie had incredible endurance, sometimes playing more than 45 minutes in a single game when other skilled players would play only 25 minutes.

In a career that spanned six decades, Gordie Howe played on 21 all-star teams, won the Art Ross trophy as the NHL's highest scorer six times, the Hart Trophy for NHL Most Valuable Player (MVP) four times, and the Stanley Cup four times. At the end of his career, Mr. Hockey retired holding just about every scoring record there was, and although Wayne Gretzky later broke many of them, Howe still holds the record for most goals scored in a career combining NHL and WHA totals. In his career Gordie Howe scored 975 goals, while Wayne Gretzky's combined totals equal 931. Truly, if even The Great One couldn't catch that record, Mr. Hockey's feat will stand for many more years to come.

nine

9

A player gets a "point" for either scoring a goal or assisting on another player's goal. To be credited with an assist, a player must have been one of the last two players to touch the puck on the team that scores the goal. Up to two assists can be given out, but if only one other player touched the puck before the goal scorer, only one assist will be awarded. Similarly, if none of his teammates touched the puck before a player scores a goal, no assists will be credited.

A beloved captain of the Toronto Maple Leafs, and a player respected around the league, Darryl Sittler enjoyed a remarkable NHL career that spanned 15 years; however, he may best be remembered by hockey fans for his heroics in a single game. In a match against the Boston Bruins on February 7, 1976, Sittler recorded two assists in the first period, three goals and two assists in the second period, and three more goals in the third period. Those 10 points broke the previous record for points in a game held by Maurice Richard, and remain as the record to this day.

ten
10

It must have been a magical night for Toronto Maple Leaf fans. Darryl Sittler scored 10 points in one game while the crowd cheered in the stands.

When a team wins the Stanley Cup every player gets to spend a day with the huge trophy. Some players invite their families and friends to a party where the cup is the centrepiece, others take it to a public event so fans can see the cup up close, and personal, and others just spend quiet time at home with the trophy. Although they have to give the Stanley Cup back at the end of the day, each player gets a miniature version of the cup to keep to commemorate the championship season.

Incredibly, Henri Richard won the Stanley Cup 11 times in his career—more than any other player in history. Richard, who is the younger brother of another hockey legend, Maurice Richard, played his entire 20-year NHL career with the Montreal Canadiens. Henri was named captain of the Canadiens in 1971, succeeding the great Jean Beliveau. Henri played in four all-star games in his career and won the Bill Masterson trophy recognizing his dedication to hockey and perseverance. In 1979 Henri was inducted into the Hockey Hall of Fame.

Henri Richard is the player who has won the most of all. Winner of **11** Stanley Cups— go see his picture at the Hall.

eleven

11

When teams play at even strength
how many will there be?
12 Add up all the players and sticks;
of each is what you'll see.

"Even strength" means both teams are playing without having anyone in the penalty box. When this is the case, each team is allowed five players and one goalie on the ice at a time. Can you count the players in the painting? Including the goalies, I bet you counted 12! Now if one of the players got a penalty and had to sit in the penalty box there would be one less player on the ice. Place your hand over one of the players in the picture and count again. How many do you count? 11! That's how many players are on the ice when one player has a penalty! Of course, each player carries one stick, so the number of players and sticks is usually the same —unless a player breaks a stick, and then there is one more player than stick on the ice. To get a new stick the player has to skate back to the bench where one of the team's trainers will usually have a stick waiting. But sometimes there's not enough time to get his own stick so a player will borrow one of his teammate's sticks until there is a break in the play.

twelve
12

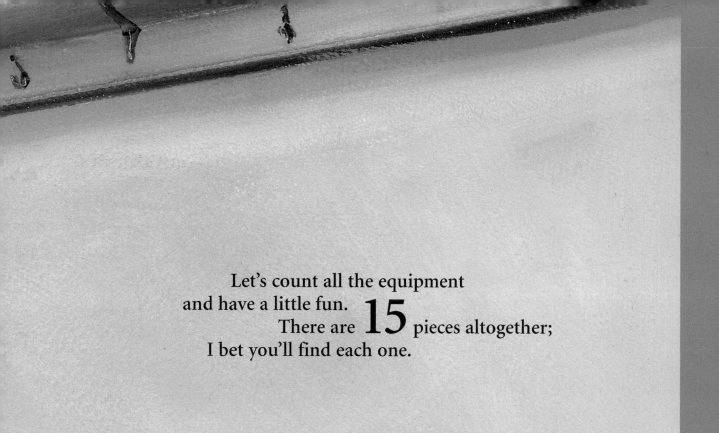

Let's count all the equipment
and have a little fun.
There are **15** pieces altogether;
I bet you'll find each one.

Hockey is a fast game and it is important to make sure your equipment fits properly so you don't get hurt! Obviously, you can't play hockey without a stick or skates, but what about some of the other pieces of equipment you can't see under the jersey? Can you find the shoulder pads, shin pads, and elbow pads in this painting? Here is a list of the 15 pieces of equipment in the illustration. Can you find them all?

A pair of skates, player stick, neck guard, a pair of gloves, pants, two goalie pads, goalie catcher, goalie blocker, goalie chest protector, goalie stick, goalie mask, and player shoulder pads.

Another fun fact for the number **15** involves a hockey record that will be very difficult to beat. In his career, Wayne Gretzky had **15** seasons in which he scored 100 or more points—a feat he accomplished more times than anyone else in history.

fifteen
15

Cammi Granato is the all-time leading scorer of the USA Women's national team. She captained both the 1998 and 2002 Women's Olympic teams in which the U.S. won gold and silver medals, respectively. At the 1998 Olympic Games in Nagano she was given the incredible honour of carrying the U.S. flag at the closing ceremonies. She is also the only American player to have played in every Woman's World Championship, including the 2005 tournament in which the Americans won the gold medal, and is considered one of the best females to ever play the game.

twenty

20

If you take the number **20**,
add "1" for being the best—
on Cammi Granato's sweater you'll see
21 for the U.S.!

Every year the Canadian Broadcasting Corporation (CBC) goes coast to coast on Saturday night with *Hockey Night in Canada* around 25 times during the regular season. The great broadcaster Foster Hewitt called the first *General Motors Hockey Broadcast,* which later became *Hockey Night in Canada,* on November 12, 1931. The early games were broadcast on the radio because TV had not even been invented! The first televised *HNIC* broadcast is said to be a Montreal Canadiens game televised on October 11, 1952.

Along with Foster Hewitt, HNIC's on-air personalities have been some of most recognized people in Canada. Foster's son Bill called games for many years until he retired in 1973. Other great *HNIC* personalities include Dick Irvin Jr., whose father won Stanley Cups as coach of both the Leafs and the Canadiens. Of course, no Saturday night would be complete without the colourful duo of Don Cherry and Ron MacLean whose intermission show, *Coaches Corner,* often draws more viewers than the game itself. Cherry has been known to get himself into trouble with his strongly voiced pro-Canadian opinions, but it is also that sense of Canadian pride and heritage (not to mention his flair for flashy suits) which won him a spot as one of CBC's top 10 *Greatest Canadians* of all time.

twenty-five

25

Close to **25** games each season are aired
for a Saturday tradition.
It's *Hockey Night in Canada* folks!
Just turn on your television.

Simply put, Scotty Bowman is the most successful coach in NHL history. Scotty began his amazing career in St. Louis, leading the expansion Blues to the cup finals in their first three seasons in the league. In Montreal, Scotty coached the Canadiens to five Stanley Cups, including four in a row, before heading to Buffalo. After leading the Sabres to two of their most successful seasons in history, Scotty moved to Pittsburgh where he was part of a Penguins team which captured two cups (one as a coach and one as Director of Player Development). Prior to his retirement in 2002, Scotty coached the Detroit Red Wings for seven years, where he became the first coach in history to lead three different teams to the Stanley Cup, capturing three more titles. Incredibly, Scotty amassed 1,244 regular season wins as a coach, far and away the most in league history—Al Arbour is second with 781. Scotty remains close to the game even after his retirement, acting as a consultant for the Red Wings.

thirty
30

Year

| 1 | 2 | 3 | 4 | 5 | 6 | 7 | 8 | 9 | 10 | 11 |

For **30** years behind the bench
one man has done the most.
Scotty Bowman has won more Stanley Cups
than any other coach can boast.

Year

13   14   15   16   17   18   19   20   21   22   23   24   25   26   27   28   29   30

Look closely at this picture now.
How many players can you find?
Each team dresses 20
which equals **40** all combined.

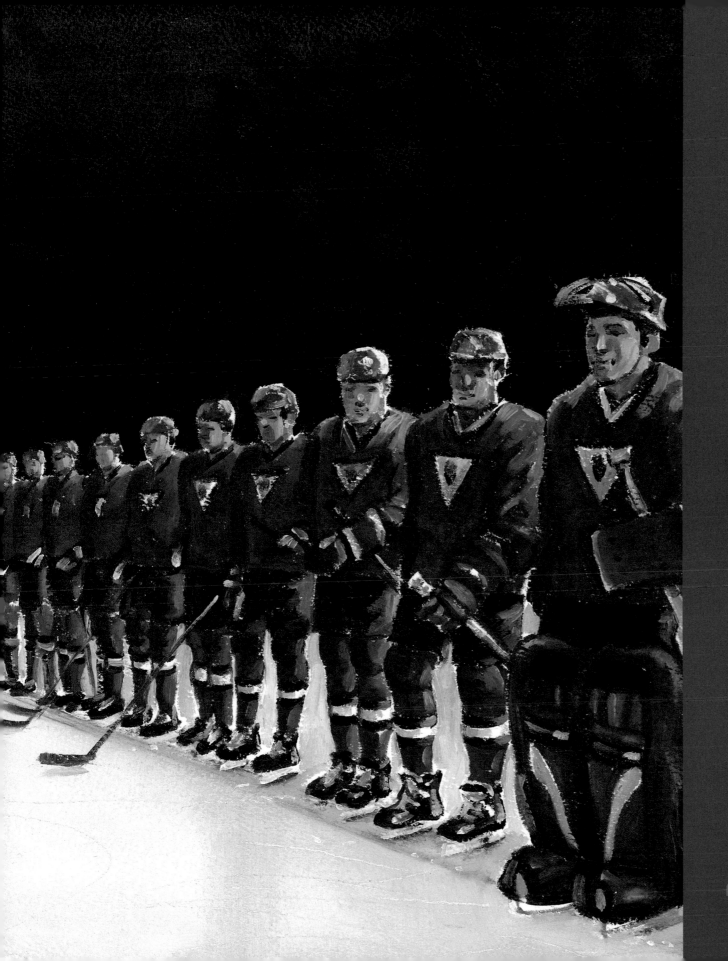

Although for the most part the NHL, Olympics, and World Hockey Championships play by very similar rules, there are some minor differences. For example, international hockey games are supposed to be played on an ice surface that is exactly 100 feet by 200 feet, whereas NHL rinks do not have a standardized size and are often smaller than the international dimensions. However, one rule each of these organizations have in common is the number of players allowed to dress for each game. Each team is allowed to have 18 players and 2 goalies in uniform every game—that means 20 players total. When you consider that two teams play each game, you can see a total of 40 players dressed, combined.

At the end of the Olympics, you can see all 40 players standing at the blue lines while the national anthem of the winning team is played. In fact, before all NHL games the national anthem is played. Many people believe the practice originated in baseball in 1918. Some teams spontaneously stood and sang the "Star Spangled Banner" during the 7th inning stretch. It is generally believed that singing the national anthem at hockey games first became common during World War II as a way for players and fans to show their patriotism. The practice has continued ever since.

forty
40

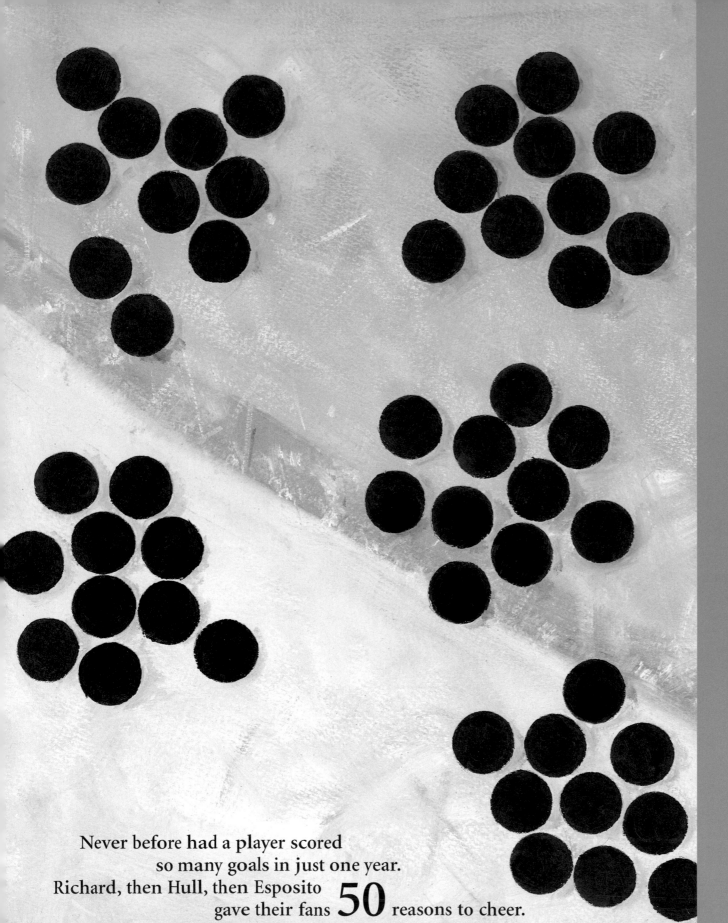

Although some had come close, no player had scored 50 or more goals in a single season until Maurice "The Rocket" Richard was able to score exactly 50 in the 1944-45 season. More than that, he was able to reach the milestone in just 50 games, a record for scoring proficiency which would not be equaled until Mike Bossy was able to do it in 1980-81—over 35 years later!

Another great goal scorer, Phil Esposito, was the first player to score 50 goals three seasons in a row, and finished his career with seven 50 or more goal seasons. The "Golden Jet" Bobby Hull, whose powerful slapshot was feared by goalies and who first developed the curved hockey stick, was the first player in league history to score more than 50 goals in a season during the 1965-66 campaign.

As remarkable as each of these accomplishments are, the traditional expectations all changed when Wayne Gretzky entered the league. In 1981-82 Gretzky scored 50 goals in just the first 39 games! Wayne Gretzky and Mike Bossy share the NHL record for the total number of 50 or more goal seasons in a career, with nine each.

fifty
50

Never before had a player scored
so many goals in just one year.
Richard, then Hull, then Esposito
gave their fans **50** reasons to cheer.

PERIOD

20+20+20=

61

In the Olympics, World's, or NHL
the time clock reads the same.
Three periods of 20 minutes each
totals **60** minutes in one game.

Every major tournament or professional hockey game consists of three 20-minute periods for a total of 60 minutes of regulation time. However, if a game is tied at the end of the 60 minutes, the teams must play overtime to determine a winner. Different leagues have different overtime rules. For example, in the play-offs the NHL plays "sudden death" overtime until a team wins. This means that the first team to score a goal wins the game and there is no time limit on the overtime. The teams keep playing extra 20-minute periods until there is a winner. In the Olympics, a winner may be determined by a shoot-out if there is still no winner at the end of an overtime period. A shoot-out means that each team picks five players to each take a breakaway, one at a time against, the other team's goalie. Whichever team scores the most shoot-out goals at the end of five breakaways wins the game.

One other difference between NHL and International games is the way time is counted. In the NHL the clock counts each period down from 20 minutes to zero, while International clocks count up from zero to 20 minutes.

sixty
60

The Montreal Canadiens, New York Islanders, and Edmonton Oilers defined two decades of NHL dominance. The 1970s belonged to the Canadiens led by the likes of Guy Lafleur, Ken Dryden, Bob Gainey, Steve Shutt, Yvan Cournoyer, Serge Savard, Guy Lapointe, Larry Robinson, Jacques Lamaire, and was coached by Scotty Bowman—every last one of whom is in the Hall of Fame. The Montreal Canadiens won six Stanley cups in the '70s, more than any other team in any other decade in the history of the NHL.

seventy
70

A decade consists of 10 long years
and with time and sweat and tears
great hockey teams were built to win
consistently with ease.

One "dynasty" ruled the 70s—
The 80s Les Canadiens of Montreal.
The 80s saw two great teams
who always won it all.

Now add 10 more...

The Edmonton Oilers and the New York Islanders owned the '80s. New York won four straight Stanley Cups from 1980 to 1984. The team, which was led by Mike Bossy, also included Hall of Famers Clarke Gillies, Denis Potvin, Billy Smith, and Bryan Trottier. Edmonton won four Stanley cups and added one more in 1990. The team was of course led by Wayne Gretzky, with a host of talented players surrounding him including Jarri Kurri, Grant Fuhr, Mark Messier, Glen Anderson, and Paul Coffey. The teams were coached by Glen Sather and John Muckler.

In 2003 many of the legends from the Canadiens and Oilers reunited to play an outdoor game called the *Heritage Classic.* The event consisted of two games. The first was the "legends" game, played by retired hockey greats, and the second was played between the current NHL Canadiens and Oilers. Despite almost minus 30 degree Celsius (-22°F) temperatures, fans packed the converted football stadium in Edmonton to watch the games, shattering the record for most fans at a live hockey game, with 57,167 fans present.

eighty
80

Everyone knows it's really hard
to net 50 goals a year.
Astonished fans watched Gretzky
give them 90 reasons to cheer.

In the same year that Wayne Gretzky scored 50 goals in the first 39 games of the season, he also set the NHL record for most goals in a single season with 92. That amazing accomplishment shattered the previous mark of 76 set by Phil Esposito in 1970-71, a record many people thought would never be broken. Since Gretzky set the record a few players have come close, but none have been able to match his 92 goals. In fact, the player who has come closest to breaking the record was Gretzky himself in 1983-84 when he scored 87 goals. Brett Hull and Mario Lemieux are the next closest with 86 and 85 goals, respectively.

ninety
90

In 971 career games Terry Sawchuk recorded 103 shutouts. That's more than one shutout every 10 games and more than any other goalie in the history of the NHL! He is remembered best for his time in Detroit. Spanning a 21-year career, Sawchuk spent the better part of 14 seasons with the Red Wings, leading them to three Stanley Cups, and claiming three Vezina trophies as the league's best goalie. He won his fourth cup and Vezina while playing for the Toronto Maple Leafs. Terry Sawchuk was inducted into the Hockey Hall of Fame in 1971, just a year after his death.

No other goalie can claim at least 100 career shutouts, but some have come close. George Hainsworth finished his career with 94, while Glen Hall and Jacques Plante had 84 and 82, respectively. Vladislav Tretiak, perhaps the best goalie to never play in the NHL, dominated international play for about 10 years—winning three Olympic gold medals and 10 World Championships, among many other accolades. How many shutouts would Tretiak have had if he played in the NHL?

Phil Esposito was the first player to score over 100 points in 1969, and Mario Lemieux is second on the all-time list, with 10 100+ point seasons. Wayne Gretzky holds the record of 100+ point seasons at 15.

one
hundred
100

100 is a milestone
to those who stop the puck.
No goalie has more shutouts
than the talented Terry Sawchuk

Matt Napier

Matt Napier was born in Montreal, Quebec, and moved frequently throughout North America and Italy with his family before settling in Ontario. He currently attends law school at the University of Windsor. Matt spends his free time reading, playing hockey, practicing guitar, and travelling. Matt enjoys visiting schools and sharing his first book *Z is for Zamboni: A Hockey Alphabet.*

Melanie Rose

Melanie lives in Mississauga, Canada, with her son Liam and their two cats, Mickey and Meesha. *Hat Tricks Count* is Melanie's eighth title with Sleeping Bear Press. She also illustrated *Z is for Zamboni: A Hockey Alphabet; M is for Maple: A Canadian Alphabet; A is for Algonquin: An Ontario Alphabet; W is for Wind: A Weather Alphabet; K is for Kick: A Soccer Alphabet; H is for Home Run: A Baseball Alphabet;* and *The Gift of the Inuksuk.* Melanie is a graduate of the Ontario College of Art.

Canadian Spelling	*American Spelling*
centrepiece	centerpiece
colourful	colorful
honour	honor
travelling	traveling